FRIENDS
OF ACPL

j975.5
Steen, Sandra.
Colonial Williamsburg

COLONIAL WILLIAMSBURG

COLONIAL WILLIAMSBURG

DILLON PRESS
New York

Maxwell Macmillan Canada
Toronto
Maxwell Macmillan International
New York   Oxford   Singapore   Sydney

by Sandra Steen
and Susan Steen

Photo Credits

Cover photo: Colonial Williamsburg Foundation
Back photo: Jamestown – Yorktown Foundation

Colonial Williamsburg Foundation: frontispiece, 21, 23, 25, 33, 34, 46, 47, 50, 52, 54, 57, 59, 63; Jamestown – Yorktown Foundation: 9, 11, 12, 15; Sandra Steen: 29; Virginia State Library & Archives: 41; Virginia State Library & Archives (special permission for use from U.S. Army Transportation Center, Fort Eustis, VA): 37

Library of Congress Cataloging-in-Publication Data

Steen, Sandra.
    Colonial Williamsburg / by Sandra Steen and Susan Steen. — 1st ed.
        p.   cm. — (Places in American history)
    Includes index.
    Summary: A look at Colonial Williamsburg, both from the historical point of view and from the viewpoint of its reconstruction so popular with tourists today.
    ISBN 0-87518-546-0
    1. Williamsburg (Va.)—History—Juvenile literature. 2. Williamsburg (Va.)—Guidebooks—Juvenile literature. [1. Williamsburg (Va.)] I. Steen, Susan. II. Title. III. Series.
F234.W7S68   1993
975.5'4252—dc20   92-26192

Dillon Press
Macmillan Publishing Company
866 Third Avenue
New York, NY 10022

Maxwell Macmillan Canada, Inc.
1200 Eglinton Avenue East
Suite 200
Don Mills, Ontario M3C 3N1

Macmillan Publishing Company is part of the Maxwell Communication Group of Companies.

First edition

Printed in the United States of America

10   9   8   7   6   5   4   3   2   1

CONTENTS

Colonial Williamsburg

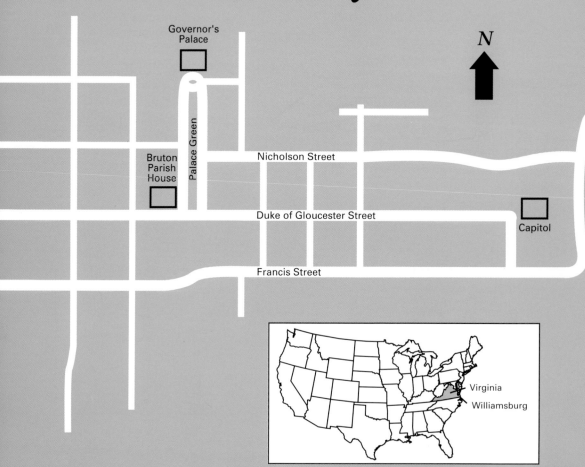

Governor's Palace

Palace Green

Bruton Parish House

Nicholson Street

Duke of Gloucester Street

Capitol

Francis Street

N

Virginia

Williamsburg

CHAPTER 1

TODAY . . . AND YESTERDAY

Step into a horse-drawn carriage in Colonial Williamsburg, the old capital of the Virginia colony, and take a ride back in time. Pass the Governor's Palace where beastlike statues guard the entrance. Then drive along Palace Green and smell roses from a garden. The bell rings in the tower of Bruton Parish Church, one of the oldest buildings in Williamsburg.

The carriage turns left onto Duke of Gloucester Street. Women wearing long dresses and men wearing wigs and short breeches enter the courthouse, shops, and taverns. Children jump into a cart pulled by oxen. As you pass Tarpley's Store, a boy runs out blowing a tin whistle.

Suddenly tourists emerge from the side door of Raleigh Tavern. The sight of them brings you back to the present time. They gobble ginger cookies. Your mouth waters, but your carriage moves on. It stops at the capitol building, where a British flag waves from the cupola, a domed tower. When you enter the Hall of the House of Burgesses, you hear men debating about taxes. You are witnessing a reenactment of history.

Colonial Williamsburg was not the first capital of Virginia. The first capital was located in a settlement six miles away on the shore of the James River. Its history began on a quiet day in May 1607. . . .

Grasping two sharp shells, a Native-American woman plucked whiskers from her husband's face. She trimmed his hair on the right side so it would not tangle in his bowstring.

Suddenly braves dashed past, shouting that ships were sailing up the river. Powhatan, chief

The Susan Constant, *along with* Godspeed *and* Discovery, *brought English settlers to the place they would soon call Jamestown.*

of the Algonquian tribes, recognized the English ships. He remembered other Englishmen who had come to explore and then moved on. He thought these new explorers would stay a short time. In a gesture of friendliness Powhatan ordered his finest braves to guide the ships to land.

The Englishmen had been sent by the Virginia Company of London to search for gold and a new route to Asia, where riches had been discovered. Although the men on ship felt weak from the foul water and lack of food, they hurried ashore. The Native Americans, with their strange-looking hair and scant clothing, frightened them. To the Native Americans, the Englishmen looked equally strange. Hair covered their faces and clothing covered most of their bodies.

Weeks earlier the Englishmen had opened a sealed box containing King James's orders. The king had named Captain John Smith as one of

Most of the wealthy gentlemen preferred to watch others build the Jamestown fort. This lack of community spirit endangered the early settlement, whose survival depended on everyone's efforts.

the seven governing councilors. The men were instructed to find a safe and healthful location and to build a settlement. They chose an inland peninsula surrounded by rivers and named the settlement Jamestown, after King James.

Most of the hundred men and four boys were unskilled or wealthy gentlemen. The few skilled men built a fort. The gentlemen either sat and watched them work or searched for gold. Before long Powhatan's enemies from a different tribe,

A reconstruction of the Jamestown settlement

attacked and killed several Englishmen. More settlers died from disease and starvation. These disasters wiped out about half the settlement.

Chief Powhatan gave food to the survivors, hoping that when the men were stronger they would return to England. He sent his men to advise the settlers. The Powhatans warned the Englishmen that wearing bright clothing made them easy targets. They advised the men to cut the tall grass around their fort so that *marrapough,* or "enemies," could not hide.

Jamestown gradually recovered as Captain Smith traded for food with tribes along the James River. While trading he demanded to know where to find gold and a passage to Asia. In return the Powhatans wanted to know how long the Englishmen planned to stay. Neither one gave honest answers.

During a winter expedition, Captain Smith claimed he was captured by Chief Powhatan's hostile brother, Opechancanough, who delivered him to Chief Powhatan. By now the chief suspected that the English planned to take over their hunting grounds. He ordered his braves to kill Captain Smith.

John Smith begged for his life. But the braves

dragged him to a rock and forced down his head. A warrior let out a blood-curdling shout and raised his club. Pocahontas, Chief Powhatan's daughter, threw herself on Captain Smith and pleaded for his life. Powhatan relented, and, as was the custom, the tribe adopted Smith.

In return Captain Smith promised the Powhatans guns. But Smith feared the Native Americans would use the guns against the settlers. He offered the Powhatans two large cannons, knowing they could not carry them to their village. So the Powhatans returned home with beads and copper.

In the fall of 1608 Captain Smith was elected president of Jamestown. He ordered the men to stop searching for gold and start planting crops to make Jamestown self-sufficient. If Smith saw men bowling instead of working, he wouldn't let them eat. When he caught men swearing, he poured cold water down their sleeves.

Opechancanough's tribe continued their

In this painting Pocahontas, daughter of Chief Powhatan, pleads for Captain Smith's life.

attacks and cut off the settler's food supplies. To keep from starving, the settlers ate cats, dogs, rats, and snakes. When these food sources ran out, some survivors dug up dead bodies and ate them.

In late 1609 an accidental gunpowder explosion burned Captain Smith, who returned to England for medical care. Without Smith's strong leadership, the settlers stopped working and Jamestown fell apart.

The remaining 60 survivors left for England.

However, as they sailed up the river, they met English ships loaded with supplies. Encouraged to stay in the New World, the settlers returned to Jamestown to rebuild the colony.

Around 1613 John Rolfe, a tobacco planter, acquired high-grade tobacco seeds from the West Indies. This plant grew so well that tobacco plantations sprang up all over the Virginia colony. Thousands of pounds of tobacco were sold to England, making planters rich.

During this time Rolfe, a widower, met Pocahontas and fell in love. A year later they married. Their marriage brought temporary peace between members of the colony and Powhatan's men.

As more and more tobacco plantations were planted, the Native Americans were forced to find new hunting grounds. To protect the remaining land from greedy invaders, the Native Americans declared war on the settlers.

In 1619 adventurers, criminals, and homeless

children arrived from England to learn a trade. Many trained as glassblowers and carpenters. These people, called indentured servants, worked for their masters for seven years to repay them for the boat fare to the New World, clothing, food, and training. In addition, Dutch traders brought kidnapped black Africans to Virginia and traded them for food. Some of these blacks became slaves and worked in the tobacco fields.

During the same year men throughout the Virginia colony elected 22 representatives known as burgesses. The Virginia Company chose a governor and six councilors. The burgesses and councilors formed the General Assembly and met in the Jamestown church twice a year to discuss laws set by England.

In 1622 hostile Native Americans attacked and destroyed many outlying settlements. Jamestown was spared. Diseases caused by swamp mosquitoes and polluted drinking water convinced some settlers to move to higher ground. In 1633 they built an outpost about six miles inland, which they called Middle Plantation.

Sixty years later James Blair, a minister, obtained a charter from England to construct a college at Middle Plantation. He accepted money from the king of England, private individuals, and imprisoned pirates who paid for their freedom. Blair named the college William and Mary, in honor of King William and Queen Mary of England.

Jamestown had flourished for 92 years as the center of Virginia life. Then one day in 1698 colonists ran toward the statehouse shouting "Fire! Fire!" The townspeople watched in horror as Jamestown's statehouse burned to the ground.

From the rubble, colonists hauled charred bricks up to Middle Plantation. There they built another statehouse and renamed the town Williamsburg, in honor of King William III.

A DAY IN COLONIAL WILLIAMSBURG

Williamsburg became the capital of the Virginia colony. By the mid-18th century its population had increased to about 1,800. Half were black slaves. Only a few residents were wealthy. The rest, called the "middling sort," operated craft shops or taverns.

Planters lived outside Williamsburg on small farms. With their slaves they planted corn and tobacco and raised animals. Two or three mornings a week farmers loaded their ox carts with milk, eggs, fruits, vegetables, and livestock. Then they drove to Williamsburg and sold their goods at Market Square, next to the courthouse.

Williamsburg housewives, cooks, and kitchen slaves pushed through crowds, bargaining for the day's eggs and butter. Flies buzzed around stalls where fish and meat were sold. Dogs barked at squawking chickens. Outside the courthouse, traders auctioned blacks into slavery.

By late morning the noise and excitement at Market Square ended. Farmers returned home to mid-afternoon dinner and their evening chores. They looked forward to Sunday, when they would attend Bruton Parish Church in Williamsburg and visit with friends.

On a typical day at a "better" house a slave entered the smokehouse. He removed a slab of meat that had been smoked over a low fire to keep it from spoiling and delivered it to another building that served as the kitchen. This detached outbuilding kept odors, excess heat, and fires from reaching the main house.

While the meat simmered in an iron pot over the fireplace, another slave made butter in a churn. The cook swung out the crane that held the pot and dropped in vegetables, stirring them

A servant presents the evening meal to a wealthy couple.

with a long-handled spoon.

Around three o'clock the cook dished the meal into covered containers. Servants carried the food to the main house and served it to the master's family. By now the food had cooled. Colonists usually ate lukewarm meals. Later the servants ate a meal of hominy grits, a kind of cornmeal.

At night a servant filled pitchers with water from the well and set one in each bedchamber. Servants warmed the bedcovers with a heated brass bedwarmer. Family members climbed into their canopied beds and closed the bed curtains to keep out drafts. There were no bathrooms in the houses, and if anyone had to go during the night, they used the chamber pot under the bed. After the family went to bed, the servants threw down their straw mattresses in attics and lofts of outbuildings. Sometimes they slept wherever they could find space.

Around six o'clock in the morning a female

Most bedchambers had few pieces of furniture, but the chamber pot was always nearby!

servant would rouse the little girl of the house, Miss Nancy, from her sleep. She poured water from the pitcher into a small china basin for Miss Nancy to bathe. Later she carried the bath water and chamber pot to the outdoor bathroom, called the "necessary house," or dumped it out the window.

Miss Nancy went downstairs and worked with her teacher. She read aloud from *Goody Two Shoes*. Girls also studied writing and some arithmetic. Boys learned the same subjects, along with Latin and Greek. Traveling teachers taught them music and dancing.

Students looked forward to one break at breakfast and another at mid-afternoon dinner. During the breaks they played marbles or a board game such as the Game of Life. They ran alongside hoops, balancing them with sticks to keep them from falling. Some children cared for their pets. Then they went back to their lessons until dark.

Balancing hoops was a favorite game of colonial children.

Parents who could afford to sent their boys to study in England or to the grammar school at the College of William and Mary, the second college built in colonial America. As young men Thomas Jefferson, John Tyler, and James Monroe attended the college and later became presidents of the United States. Other boys became apprentices and learned a trade from artisans such as carpenters and silversmiths.

Sometimes farmers hired a tutor for their children. The lessons took place in an unused tobacco field. A few Native-American boys boarded at the Brafferton School located at the college. They studied simple subjects and Christianity. Elder slaves told black children survival stories, African fables, and how to obey their master. Many children did not go to school but learned what they could from their parents.

Colonial women ran the household. During the day they shopped along Duke of Gloucester Street. Their feet sank in the soil and their shoes filled with sand. They looked over fences at beautiful gardens. Some stopped at the shoemaker's shop to pick up locally made shoes. It didn't matter which shoe went on which foot, because in the 1700s there were no right or left shoes.

In the Post Office ladies looked at books and almanacs. One lady bought *Morals and Manners.* Another picked up a letter from her cousin in England. Behind the post office Mr. Parks published the weekly *Virginia Gazette,* the first newspaper in Virginia. It reported news from Europe and carried advertisements, such as the arrival of curled wigs made of human hair or a reward for stolen horses. Mr. Parks printed books, pamphlets, and broadsides, which were notices about runaway slaves, stray cattle, lost items, and debtors.

Across the street ladies heard the clang of a blacksmith's hammer pounding metal. They headed toward the milliner's shop, where they could buy hats, fans, and gloves.

Nearby other ladies stopped at the apothecary. This shop, similar to today's drugstore, carried tobacco, herbs, spices, candy, and medicines. Shoppers could purchase sticks of slippery elm to cure sore throats or licorice sticks to brush their teeth. A small back room served as the doctor's office. Here the doctor might pull a patient's tooth or use leeches to drain blood from a black eye. More often doctors treated patients at home.

When the ladies finished shopping, they passed the courthouse, where a crowd gathered. A gentleman told them that a woman had been sentenced to the stock for disrupting the courtroom. She sat on a narrow bench made of rough wood, her legs locked through holes in a board. Another lawbreaker stood locked in a pillory, a wooden *T* with holes for arms and head. He had been caught stealing hogs.

Splat! Someone threw an egg at the man.

Crimes of swearing, stealing, and singing songs that mocked the king were punishable by serving time locked in a stock or pillory.

The crowd pointed and laughed. Perhaps the worst punishment was public humiliation.

In the evening colonists might pass a house with candles in the windows. They knew the families in these homes were celebrating a birth or anniversary. As it grew darker in Williamsburg colonists headed for taverns or home, carrying lanterns to light their way.

CHAPTER 3

FESTIVITIES AND FREEDOM

Boom! A boy covered his ears and raced toward Market Square. A firing cannon signaled the beginning of "publick times." This was when the Virginia government held court at the capitol. Every spring and fall visitors throughout the colony came to watch the court in session, but most came for parties and entertainment. They stayed at private homes, public houses, plantations, and taverns. Williamsburg's population may have tripled. At the overcrowded taverns men slept on the floor or sometimes four in a bed.

During the fair days broadsides listed the events for the day. One posted at the courthouse announced a foot race from the College of William and Mary to the capitol. The winner received a pair of silver buckles.

Visitors listened to fiddlers, and some joined the dancing, hoping to win a pair of fancy shoes. Ladies entered beauty contests. Men watched cockfights, wrestling matches, or horse races. Children laughed at puppet shows and applauded acrobats.

Stalls crammed Market Square. Merchants sold fruits, sweets, ribbons, chickens, and whistles. Craftsmen displayed their finest work.

"Pig contest!" a boy yelled. A squealing pig ran through the crowd at Market Square. Five boys chased it.

One boy grabbed the pig's tail. "I won!" he shouted. "I get to keep the pig."

At night wealthy people attended balls at the Governor's Palace or the capitol. The guests arrived in horse-drawn carriages. Gentlemen wore powdered wigs, knee-length coats, and satin knee britches. Ladies dressed in silk gowns. They took care not to get their hooped

During fair days children enjoyed puppet shows like the one above.

petticoats, called farthingales, in anyone's way.

After an elaborate feast at the Palace ball, the ladies didn't go to the powder room—the men did, where they powdered their wigs. Mean-

Palace guests dance to the music of the violin, flute, and the tinny sound of the harpsichord.

while the ladies "repaired" themselves in an upstairs bedchamber. Some ladies glued patches on their faces. These patches, shaped like stars or moons, covered smallpox scars.

Then the men escorted their wives through the double doors to the ballroom. Violin music filled the room. Ladies placed their hands on their partners' lace cuffs. They danced the minuet.

On the plantations some balls lasted for several days, so guests stayed overnight. Social dancing became so important that men often left provisions in their wills for their children to take dance lessons.

During the day visitors crowded into the capitol. They watched the House of Burgesses and the Governor's Council, known as the General Assembly, protest an unjust law set by England.

In the 13 colonies governors enforced the laws and provided protection. In 1718 the governor of North Carolina allowed pirates to raid ships off his shores, then shared the pirates' booty. The North Carolina traders pleaded with Virginia's Governor Spotswood for help. He sent two armed ships under the command of Lieutenant Maynard to capture the pirates.

Cannons roared, bullets flew, and swords clashed. Maynard faced Captain Teach, a fearsome 6' 4", 250-pound pirate known as Blackbeard. His long braided beard, woven with ribbons and slow-burning matches, must have looked frightening. With six pistols strapped to his chest, Blackbeard drew out his sword and lunged. Maynard fired his pistol. Blackbeard was shot 25 times before he finally died.

Maynard and his remaining crew returned to Williamsburg with 13 pirates in chains and Blackbeard's head hanging from the bowsprit (a mast extending from the front of a ship). After a hasty trial, the pirates were hanged.

Prisoners awaiting trial stayed in gaol, or jail, until the general court met. The jailer locked them in leg irons. The prisoners ate spoiled food and slept on straw in small unheated cells. Prisoners with money could buy better food and blankets. Those pardoned were branded on their left thumb with a *T* for thief or an *M* for mur-

The fierce pirate Blackbeard was shot 25 times before he died. His crew was taken as prisoners to Williamsburg where they were hanged for their crimes.

derer. Those not pardoned were executed at the gallows. If a slave visited a plantation without permission, he received ten lashes at the whipping post. For more severe crimes, a slave's ears were nailed to the pillory for half an hour and then cut off.

As the Virginia colony expanded westward, the number of burgesses increased. These representatives continued to meet at the capitol in Williamsburg. Their major concerns were the French and Native Americans, who refused to leave the territory of Virginia. In 1754 war broke out on the Virginia frontier. After nine years of fighting, troops from England and the colonies—including men from Virginia under the command of Lieutenant Colonel George Washington—won the war. Expenses for the war mounted, causing the British Parliament to tax the 13 colonies.

By 1774 colonists protested England's increasing taxes and the sending of troops to enforce laws. Representatives from the 13 colonies met in Philadelphia and formed the Continental Congress. Virginia sent seven representatives. One of them, Peyton Randolph of Williamsburg, was elected president of the Congress.

In 1775 Virginia representatives met in nearby Richmond. Patrick Henry thought England had gone too far with taxation and sending troops. "Give me liberty or give me death!" he shouted. Many colonists agreed. They wanted to be free of British rule. The colonists formed an army to protect themselves from British troops.

During early May 1776, Virginia representatives debated at the capitol building in Williamsburg and voted for independence from England. They wanted their colony to become a state with its own government. By June of 1776, representatives had written a plan for a new state government known as the Virginia Constitution.

At a meeting of the Continental Congress in Philadelphia, Richard Henry Lee, a Virginia representative, informed the congress that

Virginia had declared independence from England. He urged the colonies to unite and declare their independence. Before making a decision, the representatives from the other 12 colonies returned home to discuss independence. Meanwhile, Congress appointed a committee headed by Thomas Jefferson to write the Declaration of Independence. On July 4, 1776, the Continental Congress officially adopted the document, and the 13 colonies became 13 states.

In Williamsburg the Bruton Parish Church bell rang to announce independence. Even though the Declaration of Independence stated that all men are free and equal, it did not include slaves and women.

The Revolutionary War continued. When Thomas Jefferson became governor, he decided that Williamsburg was too close to the ocean and thus in danger of British attacks. He and the General Assembly agreed to move the capital to Richmond in 1780.

A painting of George Washington and other patriots discussing independence.

Shortly afterward, British troops invaded Williamsburg. In June 1781 they camped on the Palace Green and college grounds for ten days. The soldiers looted houses and refused to pay for meals at the taverns.

After the British troops left, General Washington arrived in Williamsburg. The American and French troops, along with French General Lafayette, who served with Washington, greeted him. Then Washington and his generals worked on a plan to defeat English troops at nearby Yorktown.

While fighting raged in Yorktown, the

Governor's Palace served as a hospital for wounded soldiers, and its gardens were turned into burial grounds. The effects of the war left Williamsburg in shambles.

Since Williamsburg was no longer the seat of government, its importance began to decrease. In 1824 the city briefly came alive when General Lafayette revisited and attended a banquet in his honor at Raleigh Tavern.

After many quiet years Williamsburg suddenly awoke to sounds of gunfire as the War Between the States (the Civil War) moved toward the city. During two rainy days in May of 1862, townspeople gathered with their umbrellas to watch the Battle of Williamsburg.

Due to lack of funds, the College of William and Mary was closed from 1881 to 1888. As Williamsburg entered the 20th century, it could not compete with prosperous cities like Boston and Philadelphia. With many of its buildings in ruins, Williamsburg's future as an important city looked hopeless.

CHAPTER 4

A DREAM COMES TRUE

In 1926 Dr. William A. R. Goodwin, the minister of Bruton Parish in Williamsburg, strolled with a gentleman down Duke of Gloucester Street. Weather and neglect had deteriorated the buildings over the past 145 years. Dr. Goodwin remembered as a boy buying the book *Hidden Cities Restored* and rereading it many times. Goodwin's dream was to restore 18th-century Williamsburg.

His friend supported Goodwin's vision. But the project and donations needed to be kept a secret for the time being.

During the night architects measured the streets and lots. Photographers took pictures from the air. They matched their findings with the buildings on a map drawn by a French officer in 1782.

Dr. Goodwin used the information to buy land and buildings with the donations. At the same time the Colonial Williamsburg Foundation was formed to organize and operate the historical project. By law, when Dr. Goodwin transferred the property to the Foundation, he had to reveal the millionaire's name. Dr. Goodwin announced, "Our benefactor is John D. Rockefeller, Jr."

As the project progressed, the Foundation offered to relocate families and businesses outside the historic site. Wrecking crews knocked down 600 buildings, and carpenters restored 88 original buildings. In one case a gas station was converted to its original use—the Prentis general store.

Historians studied maps, court records, journals, and other sources for authenticity. A 1740 engraved copperplate from England pictured Williamsburg buildings and plants. Detailed inventories of Wetherburn Tavern listed among its contents 19 beds and 13 slaves. A floor plan sketched by Thomas Jefferson showed exact measurements of the Governor's Palace. At the bottom of wells, archaeologists found shoes, spoons, and broken tools.

Researchers combed the United States, England, and France for original furnishings. When items could not be found, artisans reproduced originals using tools and techniques of the 18th century. Like pieces of a puzzle, the results of the research fit together to re-create Colonial Williamsburg. However, at first only the pieces that pictured Williamsburg as a rich, white community were chosen. Left out were the pieces that showed how rural families, women, and slaves really lived. Since the late 1970s these pieces have gradually been added to the puzzle to make a truer picture of Colonial Williamsburg.

Today costumed interpreters and craftsmen share the past with visitors as they did when

(opposite and above) After restoration by the Colonial Williamsburg Foundation, the Crump house looks much as it did in the 1800s.

Colonial Williamsburg opened in 1934. They tell about daily and social life and the political history that helped shape America. Visitors watch craftsmen such as blacksmiths forge nails and tools or coopers assemble barrels just as they did in the 18th century. They explain their craft and answer questions. Finished products are used or sold in the historic site.

When you visit Williamsburg you will find

two kinds of interpreters. One is a character interpreter, who pretends to be a real person living in the 18th century. He or she speaks in the first person using the word "I." If a man interprets Peter Pelham, he might say, "I am the gaoler and church organist. Every Sunday I bring a prisoner to Bruton Parish Church with me. He pumps the organ while I play."

The other interpreters speak in the third person. They tell you about people and the past. A visit to the wig shop might go like this:

"Good morning and welcome to the peruke-maker's shop," the interpreter says. "*Perruque* is a French word for "wig." In Colonial Williamsburg it was fashionable for a gentleman to wear a wig. Only wealthy men could afford wigs. A wig cost two or three pounds, the amount a craftsman earned in a month.

"After the gentleman's head was shaved, the wigmaker measured his skull. He gave the measurements to a cabinetmaker, who later carved a blockhead identical to the man's skull to hold the wig. The gentleman owned the blockhead, but it stayed in the shop ready for fittings. Meanwhile the gentleman covered his bald head with a negligee cap, a silk cap that we wore proudly in public.

"Expensive wigs were made from imported human hair. Cheaper wigs were made of goat, horse, or yak hairs." The interpreter holds up samples of hair. "Then the hair was woven on a tress loom, several strands at a time. The strands were sewn onto a caul, a cap made of linen and satin straps."

"How did they curl the wigs?" a woman asks.

The interpreter hands a white object to the visitor. "To make the wig curly, hair was rolled on paper dipped in sugar water and wrapped around one of these clay curlers. Each curler was tied with a string. For longer-lasting curls, the wig with its curlers was wrapped in cheese-cloth and put inside a loaf of unbaked bread. The

A wigmaker interpreter demonstrates the tress loom, one of the steps in making a wig.

bread was baked for a couple of hours. The moist heat set the curls."

"What happens when their hair grows back?" a visitor asks. "Does the wig still fit?"

"The men had to shave their heads almost every day," the interpreter says. "Perspiration made the caul fit tightly on their bald heads. When the wig was too tight, a man got a headache. If it was too loose, his wig would fall off."

The visitors laugh.

Interpreters invite visitors to ask questions, handle objects, and interact during the presentation.

To become an interpreter, qualified men and women attend classes to learn about the history of Williamsburg. Beginning craftsmen receive on-the-job training as apprentices just like they did in the 18th century. After six years of perfecting a skill, an apprentice may qualify as a journeyman and finally as a master craftsman. Interpreters and craftsmen continually read and research to add information to their presentations.

Children interpreters work in the summer, on weekends, or at special events. They portray family life, play a musical instrument, dance reels, or care for animals.

Visitors can see teenage boys march with drums and fifes. The boys lead the militia, or army corps. They learn to play high, short notes on the fife or long beats on the drum. In the 18th century these sounds signaled the soldiers to

Interpreters can be children, too. Here teenage boys march while playing the drums and fife.

march, turn, attack, or retreat. During battles the signals could be heard over musketfire and the roar of cannons.

Since 1926 more than $80 million has been spent on restoring Colonial Williamsburg. Donations and sales of tickets continue to finance research and operate new programs.

The early vision of a perfect town with rich, white residents no longer exists. Today Colonial Williamsburg looks lived in, with chipped paint on the houses and horse manure in the streets. Special programs focus on women, patriots, religion, health, and black history. Visitors no longer have to ask "Where are the slaves?"

CHAPTER 5

VISIT THE PAST

Colonial Williamsburg is open all year. At the Visitor Center pick up a copy of the *Visitor's Companion* for up-to-date information and a map. Some events require tickets. Others are free. Passes last a year, giving visitors a chance to return, since there are many sights to see.

Start at the reconstructed Governor's Palace. As you walk through the entrance, look at the ceiling. Weapons arranged in a circular pattern represent the power the governor had over the colonists. Don't miss the leather wallpaper, the display of firearms and swords along the stairway, and the pea-green and white bedchamber. In the dining room the table is set for an elegant supper. Notice the variety of meat dishes.

Try to visit one of the homes of a wealthy family, like George Wythe's or Peyton Randolph's. Wythe, a lawyer, Thomas Jefferson's professor, and a signer of the Declaration of Independence, lived in a beautiful house. You can tour his original brick house, gardens, and outbuildings that resemble a small plantation.

Turning left from the Palace Green onto Duke of Gloucester Street, you see the Geddy House, with a small balcony above the front door. James Geddy, a silversmith, sold his wares in a shop attached to his house. After learning about the Geddy family, go outside to the foundry, where craftsmen cast candlesticks, silverware, keys, and plates from pewter, bronze, and silver. In the 1700s silversmiths recycled gold shavings off the floor into new wares.

As you approach the reconstructed Mary Smith shop, stop and listen. You may hear the rich tones or a violin, the high notes of a flute, and the strange, tinny sound of a harpsichord, a

The entrance hall of the Governor's Palace. Note the circular display of weapons, representing the Governor's power over the colonists, on the ceiling.

pianolike instrument. Inside, interpreters are playing chamber music for a group of tourists. According to colonial rules, ladies were not allowed to play instruments that caused them to distort their faces, move in exaggerated ways, or show their elbows.

Interpreters in this shop also give lessons in proper courtesies. In colonial times girls knew how to hold fans, and boys knew how to tip their tricorn (three-cornered) hats. Visitors can learn how to curtsy and bow. Don't be shy when interpreters ask you to join in and learn the steps to a country dance. It's all part of the fun of re-creating history.

Peek in the window of the Margaret Hunter shop, a clothing and accessory store. Straw hats, gloves, and jewelry are displayed on a long counter. Shelves and drawers are filled with ribbons, fans, purses, and waistcoats.

Inside this original building visitors get a feel of how people shopped in the 1700s. There

To get a feel for the past children try on colonial clothing.

are no racks or hangers here. Shopkeepers spent time with each customer, discussing Europe's latest fashions, showing bolts of fabric, and taking measurements. Interpreters explain that several women sewed each dress, completing each in three days.

Since fabric was imported and expensive, colonists added accessories to their clothes instead of having new clothes made. A gentleman could purchase a shoe buckle or handkerchief. A lady might order a "stomacher," a new front for an old dress. Many ladies desired the latest accessory, a mirrored fan. A young lady used the fan for flirting: When she walked away from a young gentleman, she looked in her mirror to see his reaction.

Across the street at Wetherburn's Tavern, an original building, interpreters share information about Henry Wetherburn's family and the operation of his tavern. In the outbuildings history comes alive as black interpreters explain slave

A re-creation of how slaves spent their spare time with families and friends

life. Sarah tells how she manages the dairy and laundry and keeps after Tom and Rachel, who empty chamber pots and make the beds.

On Saturday nights slaves spent time with their families and friends. For entertainment, men played the banjo or fiddle, while others sang and danced. On Sundays they attended Bruton Parish Church, sitting in their pews apart from the whites. After church they socialized and caught up on the latest news.

Don't leave Williamsburg without seeing a blacksmith make 18th-century tools and hoes. Be sure to mail a postcard at the post office. Then go outside and downstairs to the printing office and watch a craftsman ink the press to print a copy of the *Virginia Gazette*. Next door observe apprentices demonstrate book binding.

Visit the cooper, where a craftsman makes wooden barrels, tubs, and pails. Spend time inside the Magazine, an original octagonal-shaped building, which displays 18th-century firearms and military equipment. Across town at Robertson's mill stands a reconstructed windmill, which grinds corn. Next to the windmill characters interpret rural trades. A basket-maker splits a log to form strips for weaving baskets and chairs.

At the east end of Duke of Gloucester Street stands the reconstructed capitol. In the H-shaped building the Governor and his council met on

one side and the House of Burgesses on the
other. When the two groups disagreed about a
law, they met in the middle of the H, upstairs in
the conference room. Sit on a bench and imagine
Patrick Henry and Thomas Jefferson fighting for
independence.

After a visit to Colonial Williamsburg, you
might enjoy a day at nearby Jamestown settlement. Stop at the re-created Powhatan long-
houses, where costumed interpreters cook and
make tools while they explain Native-American
life. Down the path you'll find a reproduction of
the Jamestown fort. Inside you'll observe and
talk to interpreters, who act as early settlers. As
you walk around the fort, watch out for stray
chickens. Take time to try on the armor. At the
dock climb aboard a replica of the ship *Susan
Constant* and listen to a sailor tell about his trip
to the New World.

During the year Jamestown settlement
offers programs for all ages. Parents and children

may dig for artifacts, design a pot to take home, or learn about Native-American hunters and make a hunting headdress. In September families join in the games and entertainment at the Jamestown Children's Festival or celebrate a Jamestown Christmas in December.

In Colonial Williamsburg children and families choose from a variety of exciting activities throughout the year. They may enlist in a military encampment. Here they are assigned to tents, carry guns, learn to march together, and fire cannons. Young visitors may grind corn at the mill, make bricks, bowl, watch artisans at work, or learn about livestock. For entertainment, they listen to storytellers or watch puppet shows.

Whether you observe or participate, learn or be entertained, Colonial Williamsburg offers something for everyone. This living museum shares the history of Native Americans, European immigrants, and African slaves who

In this fire drill children pass water buckets to re-create a colonial fire brigade. Colonial Williamsburg invites visitors to participate and learn how their ancestors lived.

created America. The Colonial Williamsburg Foundation strives to set an example of an authentic and changing Colonial Williamsburg, with the hope that visitors leave with a sense of their motto: "What can the future learn from the past?"

Colonial Williamsburg: A Historical Time Line

1607 Captain John Smith and the men of the Virginia Company arrive from England and settle in Jamestown.

1619 A General Assembly is formed at Jamestown.

1622 The Virginia colony is nearly destroyed by Native Americans.

1633 Middle Plantation, near Jamestown, is established.

1693 The College of William and Mary is founded at Middle Plantation.

1716 First American playhouse is built in Williamsburg.

1718 Blackbeard's men are tried and hanged in Williamsburg.

1736 William Parks prints the first public newspaper, the *Virginia Gazette*.

1774 The Continental Congress, made up of 13 colonies, is formed.

1776 The Virginia Constitution is written.

1779 Thomas Jefferson becomes governor of Virginia.

1780 The Virginia capitol building is moved to Richmond.

1781 Williamsburg is invaded by the British.

1824 French General Lafayette revisits Williamsburg.

1863 Battle of Williamsburg is fought during the Civil War.

1881– College of William and Mary is closed due
1888 to lack of funds.

1926 Dr. William A. R. Goodwin and John D. Rockefeller, Jr., begin plans to restore Williamsburg.

1934 Restored Colonial Williamsburg opens to the public.

1944 President Franklin D. Roosevelt visits Colonial Williamsburg.

1957 Queen Elizabeth of England visits Colonial Williamsburg. Abby Aldrich Rockefeller Folk Art Center opens.

1964– Archaeological excavations at
1966 Wetherburn's Tavern uncover 200,000 fragments of glass, metal, and pottery.

1970s Archaeological excavations uncover slave quarters at Carter's Grove, a nearby plantation owned by the Colonial Williamsburg Foundation.

1985 The DeWitt Wallace Decorative Arts Gallery is completed. It houses 17th- to 19th-century furniture, paintings, silver, and costumes.

VISITOR INFORMATION

Colonial Williamsburg

Hours

9:00 A.M. to 5:00 P.M. every day.
General Information
> Visitors may walk the historic site and enter shopping areas free of charge. Costumed interpreters are available to answer questions. Entrance into historical buildings requires a ticket.

Visitor Center

8:00 A.M. to 7:00 P.M. daily.
> Provides tickets, bookstore, food services, theater, and rest rooms. Free copy of weekly *Visitor's Companion* includes current events, programs, times, and maps for museums, exhibitions, and historic trade sites.

Tours

Bus service: From Visitor Center 8:50 A.M. to 10:00 P.M. Ticket holders only. *Patriot Tour:* Orientation walk through the historic area. Ticket holders only. *Carriage and wagon rides:* Additional ticket needed and weather permitting. *Evening Lanthorn Tour:* Walking tour of selected trade shops. Additional ticket needed.

Special Events

January, February, March: Colonial weekends.
> *February:* Washington's Birthday weekend. *March/April:* Easter weekend. *July:* Independence Day. *Late August/ September:* Publick Times. *November:* Thanksgiving weekend. *December:* Grand Illumination and Christmas Season.

Other events of interest: "Other Half Tour" explores the

African-American point of view. "According to the Ladies"
portrays women in the 18th century. "Militia Review"
demonstrates military drills and music. Storytelling.
Events for children are listed in summer issues of
Visitor's Companion.

Jamestown Settlement

Hours

Museum: 9:00 A.M. to 5:00 P.M., except Christmas and
New Year's Day. *Powhatan Indian Village, James Fort,
ship replicas:* 9:00 A.M. to 5:00 P.M., except Christmas Day.
Closed the months of January and February.

Visitor Services

Provides tickets and information: gift/bookstore, rest
rooms, and food services.

Special Events

Admission charged.

March: Military through the Ages. *May:* Jamestown
Landing Day. *June:* Virginia Indian Heritage Festival.
September: Jamestown Children's Festival. *November:*
Foods and feasts in 17th-century Virginia. *December:* A
Jamestown Christmas.

For more information, contact:

Jamestown Settlement
P.O. Box JF
Williamsburg, VA 23187
804–229–1607

The Colonial Williamsburg
Foundation
P.O. Box 1776
Williamsburg, VA 23187
1-800-History

INDEX